Problem
Solving Years 5-6

Pete Hall

HOPSCOTCH

A division of MA Education Ltd

Published by Hopscotch
A division of MA Education Ltd
St Jude's Church
Dulwich Road
Herne Hill
London SE24 0PB

Tel: 020 7738 5454

© 2008 MA Education Ltd

Written by Pete Hall
Series design by Blade Communications
Cover illustration by Susan Hutchison
Illustrated by Bernard Connors
Printed in the UK by CLE

ISBN 978-1-90430-719-8

Problem Solving Years 5-6

'The ability to solve problems is at the heart of mathematics.'

Mathematics Counts 1982

Problem solving has always been an important but neglected element of mathematics. Far too much of mathematics teaching concentrated on the practice and consolidation of number skills in isolation from the broader context, ie why we needed to learn the skills. The introduction of the National Curriculum for mathematics, with its emphasis on 'Using and applying', was a forward step. However, since the launch of the National Numeracy Strategy and the *Framework for Teaching Mathematics* there appears to have been a decline in the emphasis on problem solving. Indeed the HMI Evaluation of the National Numeracy Strategy (2001) reports that 'in the main teaching activity, problem solving is still underemphasised'.

This book offers 18 problem-solving lessons. Each lesson combines teaching objectives from the Solving Problems section of the *Framework for Teaching Mathematics* with objectives from the general sections. This approach will provide more time within the mathematics curriculum because objectives are combined and linked. Each lesson is aimed at providing children with a challenging learning experience with the emphasis on enjoyment. Mathematics is a wonderfully exciting and rewarding subject and it is vital as teachers that we communicate this to our children.

Problem-solving qualities

In order to make progress in problem-solving activities children need to develop a range of skills or qualities that are not specific to mathematics. Many children can find problem solving very daunting because they have not developed these necessary qualities. Therefore it is vital that schools start to develop them in Key Stage 1 and continue to develop them throughout the children's school careers. Schools should discuss how they could develop these necessary qualities, which include the following:

- The ability to discuss, work cooperatively and work individually.
- The ability to communicate using mathematics.
- The ability to define and understand problems.

- The ability to think of key questions.
- The ability to explore and experiment.
- The ability to recognise 'blind alleys'.
- The ability to develop 'transfer skills'.
- The ability to use imagination and flexibility of mind.
- The ability to be reflective.
- The ability to persevere.

Mathematical problem-solving skills

In addition to the generic qualities listed above, the National Curriculum lists these skills.

Using and applying number

Pupils should be taught to:

Problem solving

a) Make connections in mathematics and appreciate the need to use numerical skills and knowledge when solving problems in any other parts of the mathematics curriculum.
b) Break down a more complex problem or calculation into simpler steps before attempting a solution; identify the information needed to carry out the tasks.
c) Select and use appropriate mathematical equipment, including ICT.
d) Find different ways of approaching a problem in order to overcome any difficulties.
e) Make mental estimates of the answers to calculation; check results.

Communicating

f) Organise work and refine ways or recording.
g) Use notation diagrams and symbols correctly within a given problem.
h) Present and interpret solutions in the context of the problem.
i) Communicate mathematically, including the use of precise mathematical language.

Reasoning

j) Understand and investigate general statements.
k) Search for patterns and their results; develop logical thinking and explain their reasoning.

The lessons

Each lesson follows the same format.

Learning objectives

These are taken directly from the yearly teaching programmes in the *Framework for Teaching Mathematics*. The solving problems objectives are linked with at least one other objective.

Vocabulary

This lists all the appropriate words and phrases to be used in the lesson. It is vital that children should see these words as well as hear them. So either they should be written on the board or if sets of vocabulary cards are available use these.

Resources

The lessons have been written to use a minimum of resources. Most of the resources listed would be found in most primary classrooms. Some lessons have resource sheets or activity sheets that can be photocopied.

Oral and mental starter

These short sessions are intended to provide the children with a lively and fun start to the lesson. The objectives are taken from the National Numeracy Strategy's sample medium-term planning.

Teaching points

A detailed lesson plan to guide you through the lesson. The emphasis is on lively activities that will demonstrate to the children that mathematics is alive!

Plenary

All the plenaries have been planned to allow the children to reflect on what has gone before. Often there are 'challenges' included in the plenary. The principle here is to ensure that the children's ability is challenged but in a non-threatening way.

Support and Extension

These sections are aimed at supporting the less able and challenging the more able. The nature of problem solving is such that much of the work is 'open ended' and, therefore, differentiation should be more manageable.

Questions to guide assessment

Teacher assessment is an important component of teaching. These questions are included to help you focus on a small number of issues. The nature of problem solving is such that it is very difficult to make summative judgements. For example, 'Presents results in an organised way'. The child in Reception can do this in one way and a Y6 child in another way but both could be as valid. It is up to teachers to use their professional judgement through teacher assessment.

Calculators

Some of the lessons involve the use of calculators and in particular the OHP calculator. This is a very powerful learning tool for young children.

Wherever the calculator is suggested it is used to support children's learning. Therefore the approach in these books is in line with the recommendations of the National Numeracy Strategy.

Cheap travel

Framework for Numeracy objectives

Solving problems

○ Use all four operations to solve simple word problems involving numbers and quantities based on 'real life' and money using one or more steps. Explain methods and reasoning.

Calculations

○ Use informal pencil and paper methods to support, record or explain additions and subtractions. Extend written methods to column addition and subtraction of two integers less than 10,000 and addition of more than two integers less than 10,000.

○ Approximate first. Use informal pencil and paper methods to support, record or explain multiplications and divisions.

○ Extend written methods to: short multiplication of HTU, long multiplication of TU by TU and short division of HTU by U.

○ Develop calculator skills and use a calculator effectively.

○ Check with the inverse operation when using a calculator.

VOCABULARY

total, altogether, average, difference

Resources

○ Photocopiable Sheets 1 to 5 (pages 42 to 46)
○ A class set of calculators

Oral and mental starter

Objective: Add and subtract any pair of two-digit numbers, including crossing 100.

○ Give the children 'target numbers', for example 124. They have to write down as many TU and TU additions as they can that equal that number. Alternatively you can ask the children to write down, say five additions. Repeat this for other target numbers.

○ Extend this to asking the children what they would need to subtract from the target number to leave a TU number.

Problem-solving challenge

Which is the cheapest method of travel?

With the whole class

○ Give the children copies of photocopiable Sheet 1 (page 42). Read through the sheet with them, asking the children how they would fill in the answers for each section for the journey from Abouttown to Bettertown. Demonstrate on the board how to calculate the cost of each journey. Make a point of stressing the use of multiplication rather than repeated addition.

○ Ask the children to tell what 'total' means and how you calculate it. Ask the children what the term 'average' means and how you calculate it.

Children working individually

○ Give the children copies of photocopiable Sheet 2 (page 43). Tell them that this sheet is for recording their calculations for the challenges on Sheet 1 but that they should write their answers on Sheet 1.

○ Tell them to check their calculations by an appropriate method; this would include checking by using a calculator or the inverse operation. Whatever method they choose they should write the way they did it in the box.

○ Now give the children photocopiable Sheet 3 (page 44), which is the same activity but for a family of four who are doing a return journey. Let them use calculators to calculate the answers to this sheet but encourage them to check with the calculator by using the inverse operation.

Plenary

○ Ask the children what calculation methods they used to find the answers. Discuss with them how realistic they think the answers are. Explain that in real life the journey by train for four people would be a lot cheaper because train companies offer special family tickets.

○ To finish the lesson give the children some 'difference' questions to calculate in pairs. For example, 'What is the difference in miles between the distances from A to B and C to D?'

Support

○ Let the children use photocopiable Sheet 4 (page 45). This has easier calculations and therefore lets the children take part in the same type of problem but at their level.

Extension

○ The children could be set harder challenges, such as 'What would be the cost of each return journey for two families? One family has three people in it and the other has four people.'

○ The children could use the ideas on photocopiable Sheet 1 but have to design their own version of it. They have to think of the distances and costs themselves. Let them use photocopiable Sheet 5 (page 46) as a template.

Answers

Photocopiable sheet 1

Town	Town	Distance in miles	Car cost	Taxi cost	Train cost
Abouttown	Bettertown	153	13.77	30.60	7.65
Coldtown	Deartown	207	18.63	41.40	10.35
Everytown	Fasttown	504	45.36	100.80	25.20
Greattown	Hottown	801	72.09	160.20	40.05
Idealtown	Jollytown	945	85.05	189.00	47.25
		Totals	234.90	522.00	130.50
		Average Costs	46.98	104.40	26.10

Photocopiable Sheet 3

Town	Town	Distance in miles	Car cost	Taxi cost	Train cost
Abouttown	Bettertown	153	27.54	612.00	36.72
Coldtown	Deartown	207	37.26	828.00	49.68
Everytown	Fasttown	504	90.72	2016.00	120.96
Greattown	Hottown	801	144.18	3204.00	192.24
Idealtown	Jollytown	945	170.10	3780.00	226.80
		Totals	469.80	10440.00	626.40
		Average Costs	93.96	2088.00	

125.28

Photocopiable Sheet 4

Town	Town	Distance in miles	Car cost	Taxi cost	Train cost
Abouttown	Bettertown	10	.80	20.00	.50
Coldtown	Deartown	20	1.60	40.00	1.00
Everytown	Fasttown	30	2.40	60.00	1.50
Greattown	Hottown	40	3.20	80.00	2.00
Idealtown	Jollytown	50	4.00	100.00	2.50
		Totals	12.00	300.00	7.50

Questions to guide assessment

○ Did the children choose appropriate calculation methods?

○ Did the children check their calculations with an appropriate method?

○ Did the children use the calculator effectively?

Holiday on the cheap!

Framework for Numeracy objectives

Solving problems

- Use all four operations to solve simple word problems involving numbers and quantities based on 'real life' and money using one or more steps, including making simple conversions of pounds to foreign currency and finding simple percentages.
- Explain methods and reasoning.

Calculations

- Use informal pencil and paper methods to support, record or explain additions and subtractions. Extend written methods to column addition/subtraction of two integers less than 10,000 and addition of more than two integers less than 10,000. Addition or subtraction of a pair of decimal fractions.
- Approximate first. Use informal pencil and paper methods to support, record or explain multiplications and divisions.
- Extend written methods to: short multiplication of HTU, long multiplication of TU by TU and TU by T and short division of HTU by U.
- Develop calculator skills and use a calculator effectively.
- Check with the inverse operation when using a calculator.

VOCABULARY

deduct, convert, conversion, exchange rate, supplements

Resources

- Number fans
- A range of holiday brochures. (You could ask the children to get some. Ideally they should go to the travel agent's with an adult.)
- Photocopiable Sheet 6 (page 47)

Oral and mental starter

Objective: Recall addition and subtraction facts for each number up to 20.

- Give the children number fans. Set them questions such as, 'If I subtract 6 from 20, what would I add to 6 to get back to 20?' and 'I subtracted a number from 20 and I have 12 left; what was that number?'

Problem-solving challenge

Which is the cheapest holiday?

With the whole class

- Organise the children into pairs. Give each pair a travel agent's holiday brochure.

- Give the children time to look through the brochures before directing them to the sections that show the prices. Using one brochure as an example go through the 'pricing policy', ie they try to make it as complicated as they can! Explain that there are things called supplements, which have to be added to the price given in the brochure. These can be for: the time of year you go on holiday; where you fly from; how many people are in the group; whether there are children going and so on.

- Explain to the children that they are going to work out the costs of some holidays today but, luckily for them, you have invented your own hotels and prices!

- Give the children copies of photocopiable Sheet 6 (page 47). Explain that the prices given are in euros. Some explanation of the euro may be necessary and it would be ideal to show them some. Demonstrate on the board how to convert euros to pounds. If the children experience difficulty with this idea you could construct a conversion chart on the board.

    €1: £0.60   €2: £1.20   €3: £1.80

○ Rather than build up the whole chart just put up important facts like €50, €100 and so on.

○ Depending on the objectives you want to set for this lesson the children could do all the calculations with the calculator. Or you may wish to 'mix and match' the objectives and allow the children to use the calculator for some of the harder calculations.

○ Give the children these challenges.

Children working in pairs

Challenge 1

How much would it cost in pounds for one person to go for one week's holiday (Saturday to Saturday, not including the last Saturday night) in each hotel below? This person wants breakfast every day.
Answers:

> Hotel Sunny Delight – 7 nights @ €50 = €350, deduct €20 = €330 or £198

> Hotel Happy – 7 nights @ €40 = €280, add 7 breakfasts @ €7 = €49 = €329, deduct €16 = €313 or £187.80

> Hotel Goodtime – 7 nights @ €55 = €385, deduct €60 = €325 or £195

Challenge 2

How much would it cost in pounds for two people to go for a week's holiday (Saturday to Saturday, not including the last Saturday night) in each hotel? The two people want to share a double room and have breakfast every day.
Answers:

> Hotel Sunny Delight
> 7 nights @ €70 = €490, deduct €20 = €470 or £282.00

> Hotel Happy
> 7 nights @ €60 = €420, add breakfasts €98 (14 @ €7) = €518, deduct €16 = €502 or £301.20

> Hotel Goodtime
> 7 nights @ €75 = €525, deduct €60 = €465 or £279

Challenge 3

The final challenge for the children is to announce that each hotel has agreed a 10% reduction in their prices! Ask them to work out the new prices in euros.

Plenary

○ Discuss with the children why the holiday brochures are so confusing. Ask the children to discuss, in pairs, a way of pricing holidays to make it simpler to understand.

○ Take feedback from the children and discuss the merits of some of their suggestions.

Support

○ Limit the number of days that the children have to work out the price for and just ask the children to write the answer in euros and not convert the price into pounds.

Extension

○ There are many ways to extend this activity. The number of days of each holiday can be increased as can the number of people going on holiday. Increase the percentage reduction to a figure the children will find challenging. Ask the children to work out what the VAT might be on each holiday.

○ Alternatively, see if the children can use the brochures to work out the cost of a holiday for four somewhere in August, for example.

Questions to guide assessment

○ Did the children choose appropriate calculation methods?
○ Did the children check their calculations with an appropriate method?
○ Did the children use the calculator effectively?

When is a rectangle not a rectangle?

Framework for Numeracy objectives

Solving problems
○ Make and investigate a general statement about shapes by finding examples that satisfy it.
○ Explain methods and reasoning, orally and in writing.

Shape and space
○ Recognise properties of rectangles.
○ Understand and use angle measure in degrees.

VOCABULARY

diagonals, bisect, parallel, symmetry

Resources
○ Protractors or angle measures
○ Plain paper
○ Scissors
○ Rulers
○ Mirrors
○ A range of rectangles
○ Photocopiable Sheet 7 (page 48)

Oral and mental starter

Objective: Halve any two-digit number.

○ Play 'Halving bingo'. Ask the children to draw a 4 x 4 table and write in it 16 numbers below 50. Tell them that they can have halves if they want to. For example $12\frac{1}{2}$. You then start asking calculation questions such as, 'Half of 70?' and 'Half of 89?' The children have to work out the answer and if they have that number on their 'bingo card' they cross it out. The first child to complete their card wins.

Problem-solving challenge

Are all rectangles the same?

With the whole class

○ Organise the children into pairs and give each pair a copy of photocopiable Sheet 7 (page 48). Before sending them off to work in pairs, explain to them what they are going to do. They are going to read each statement on the sheet and then vote on the statement, either agreeing or disagreeing. Remind them what 'bisect' means and make sure they understand 'four lines of symmetry'. Say they are going to investigate each statement. The onus is on them to prove or disprove each statement. The way they can do this is by drawing rectangles and investigating each statement in turn. The 'proof' they offer can be mainly drawn but must have some written explanation.

○ Before they start, remind the children how to draw a rectangle using rulers and protractors.

Children working in pairs

○ As the children are investigating each statement try not to intervene unless they are going in a hopeless direction with their investigation. They will, no doubt, ask if their 'proofs' are acceptable but try not to be drawn.

○ Either stop the children after all of them have finished investigating the first statement and have a mini-plenary where the statement is discussed, or wait until everyone has investigated all the statements and discuss them in the plenary. Tell the pairs that they then have to choose one of the statements and write on the bottom part of Sheet 7 whether or not they agree with it.

Plenary

○ Use these questions to guide the plenary or the mini-plenaries you had in the main part of the lesson.

- Do you agree with the statement?
- Does anyone disagree with the statement and why?
- What kind of proof have you offered for each statement?

○ Make this statement to the children: 'All squares are rectangles'. Ask them to work in pairs to investigate this statement by drawing a square and discussing it by comparing the square to each of the statements on Sheet 7. Ask for feedback from the children.

○ If necessary, finish the lesson by telling the children that all the statements are true.

Support

○ Let the children draw around rectangles rather than draw them with a protractor.

○ Limit the statements they have to investigate to those involving angles and symmetry.

Extension

○ Ask the children to investigate the properties of other shapes, such as triangles and pentagons. Ask them to make a list of properties similar to the statements for a rectangle.

Questions to guide assessment

○ Could the children investigate each statement in a logical way?
○ Could they explain their methods and reasoning?
○ Could they draw the rectangles accurately?

Name that triangle!

Framework for Numeracy objectives

Solving problems

○ Make and investigate a general statement about shapes by finding examples that satisfy it.

○ Explain methods and reasoning, orally and in writing.

Shape and space

○ Classify triangles (isosceles, equilateral, scalene), using criteria such as equal sides, equal angles, and lines of symmetry.

VOCABULARY

isosceles, equilateral, scalene, lines of symmetry

Resources

○ Photocopiable Sheets 8 to 10 (pages 49 to 51)
○ Scissors
○ Rulers
○ Protractors
○ A range of 2D triangles

Oral and mental starter

Objective: Read and write whole numbers to at least 100,000.

○ Ask five different children to tell you a digit from 1 to 9. Write the digits on the board to make a five-digit number. The children have to work in pairs and tell each other what number it is. Repeat this process a few times.

○ Then tell the children that you are going to say a number and they have to write it down and then show each other their answer. They have to say to each other whether the answer is right or wrong. Repeat this a few times.

Problem-solving challenge

Can you name the triangle?

With the whole class

○ Ask the children to tell you the names of some triangles. At this age they will probably know the names of an equilateral triangle and an isosceles triangle. Ask them what the properties of each triangle are. (An equilateral triangle has equal angles and sides. An isosceles triangle has two equal angles and sides.) Draw these two on the board.

○ Now draw on the board a scalene triangle and tell the children its name. Ask what they can tell you about it. (It has no equal sides or angles.)

○ Do the same for a right-angled triangle.

Children working in pairs/individually

○ Give the children copies of photocopiable Sheet 8 (page 49). Tell them that they have to cut out each statement and triangle name card and then match the statements to a type of triangle. Discuss anything that needs clarification, such as what lines of symmetry are.

○ When they have done this they can be given photocopiable Sheet 9 (page 50). They now have to cut out each shape and then, using rulers and protractors, measure the angles and sides of each triangle and write the measurements on the actual triangle.

○ When the children have completed this task, explain to them that the next challenge is to record the identity of different triangles together with a general statement about each one. To do this give them copies of photocopiable Sheet 10 (page 51). They should sketch the triangle and write one statement about it.

Plenary

○ Ask the children to read out their statements about their triangles. Talk about the lines of symmetry in a triangle. For some triangles it is quite straight forward to identify lines of symmetry. How could we find a line of symmetry in a scalene triangle? Indeed, is this possible?

○ Show the children an equilateral triangle and ask them what size the angles are. Then ask them to imagine that you have made the triangle twice as large. Ask them what size the angles would be now. Repeat this for other triangles to ensure that the children understand that no matter what type of triangle, if you make it uniformly larger or smaller the angles remain the same.

Support

○ Give the children a range of triangles to sort using some, but not all, of the statements on photocopiable Sheet 8. They could be given, for example, 'All the sides are of equal length,' and they have to find as many triangles as they can that fit that criterion. Change the criteria you give the children depending on their ability.

Extension

○ Ask the children to write as many different criteria as they can for all the triangles.

Questions to guide assessment

○ Could the children classify their triangles correctly?
○ Could they write precise statements about the properties of triangles?
○ Could the children identify lines of symmetry?

Routes around school

Framework for Numeracy objectives

Solving problems

○ Use all four operations to solve simple word problems involving numbers and quantities based on 'real life' and measures, using one or more steps.

○ Explain methods and reasoning.

Measures

○ Use, read and write standard metric units (km, m, cm, mm), including their abbreviations, and understand the relationships between them.

○ Convert larger to smaller units (such as km to m, m to cm or mm).

○ Suggest suitable units and measuring equipment to estimate or measure length.

> **VOCABULARY**
>
> shortest, longest, estimate, distance

Resources

○ Photocopiable Sheets 11 to 13 (pages 52 to 54)
○ A range of measuring equipment

Oral and mental starter

Objective: Find pairs with a sum of 100.

○ Play the 'Great pairs challenge'. Tell the children they have ten minutes to write down as many pairs of whole numbers that equal 100 as they can.

○ When they have finished choose a number at random, such as 24, and ask if anyone can tell you the pair to that number in order to make 100.

Problem-solving challenge

Which is the shortest way?

Notes for the teacher

○ This lesson is different from other lessons in this book because it depends upon the school geography! The lesson objective is to set the children a measures problem that involves finding the shortest routes. All schools are designed differently but all will have some shortest route issue. A very common one is finding the shortest route to the secretary's office, so that the register is taken back efficiently. Note the emphasis is on 'shortest', not 'quickest'. We do not want to encourage children to run around the school!

○ Here are a few suggestions.
  What is the shortest route from the classroom to:
  • the headteacher's room
  • the hall
  • the dining room
  • the playground or field
  • the carpark?
  What is the shortest route to use from the classroom to the designated meeting place in the event of a fire?

○ If the school geography does not lend itself to any of these then there are two other possibilities.
  1) Mark out a challenge on the playground either using PE cones or drawn on the ground using chalk.
  2) 'Micro measuring' – measure short distances within the area of the classroom. For example, 'What is the shortest distance that Sanjit could travel to get from his seat to the cloakroom?'

Classroom organisation

○ Obviously the way this is organised will depend on the challenge selected. It may be possible for the class to be split into groups, each group taking turns to investigate the challenge. While one group investigates the problem the others can complete the photocopiable sheets. Alternatively, it may be more appropriate for one or two groups to investigate the problem during a series of lessons on measures. In this instance the photocopiable sheets could be used as an assessment activity.

○ Whichever way the measuring is organised the following format is suggested as a way forward.

With the whole class

○ Introduce the problem to the children and ask for responses. 'What do you think is the shortest route from this classroom to...?' There may need to be some discussion on defining the route. For example, they may think of a short way that involves going through a part of the school the children are not allowed in; the staff room, for example.

○ Once the parameters of the problem have been defined, discuss the issue of **how** the children are to do the measuring. Ask them what they are going to use to find the distance. If you have a range of measuring equipment in the classroom it would be worth showing the children each item and asking what they would measure with it. Try to establish what unit of measure the children think the distance should be measured in. For example, ask the children if they think it would be appropriate to measure the distance to the headteacher's room in millimetres.

Children working in groups

○ As described above, set the children to work either on the challenge described or on photocopiable Sheets 11 to 13 (pages 52 to 54), whichever is appropriate for their level of ability (see Support and Extension). On these sheets the children have to investigate routes across the page. The emphasis is on finding **their** longest and shortest routes rather than **the** longest and shortest.

Plenary

○ Establish the 'answer' to the problem. Given the nature of measuring, it is unlikely that any two groups will have the same measurement! Talk to the children about why that should be.

○ Write some of the measurements on the board and ask the children questions that involve converting the measurements to different units. For example, 'What would this be in centimetres?'

○ Are there any other shortest route problems they would like to investigate at another time?

○ Ask the children to think about challenges such as:
  • What is your shortest route home?
  • What is the shortest route to your friend's house?
  • What is the shortest route from here to London!?

Support

○ For the actual measuring there are a number of ways to do this. The children could be 'paired' with a more able child, who could help. If you have a classroom assistant, they can help with the measuring.

○ You could choose to let these children do some 'micro measuring' within the classroom.

○ Give the children photocopiable Sheet 11 to do.

Extension

○ Set the children an appropriately challenging measuring task that requires some degree of accuracy. For example, 'I want you to find the distance from A to B to the nearest centimetre.' Encourage the children to think of their own 'shortest distance' challenge.

○ The children can complete photocopiable Sheet 13.

Questions to guide assessment

○ Did the children cooperate with each other to solve the problem?
○ Could the children measure the distance with reasonable accuracy?
○ Could the children convert measurement distances?

All the fours!

Framework for Numeracy objectives

Solving problems

○ Choose and use appropriate number operations to solve problems, and appropriate ways of calculating: mental, mental with jottings, written methods and using the calculator.

Calculations

○ Understand the effects of and relationships between the four operations, and the principles (not the names) of the arithmetic laws as they apply to multiplication. Begin to use brackets.

○ Use the relationship between multiplication and division.

○ Use known facts and place value to multiply and divide mentally.

○ Develop calculator skills and use a calculator effectively.

○ Check with the inverse operation when using a calculator.

○ Check with an equivalent calculation.

VOCABULARY

more than, less than, add, subtract, equals, total

Resources

○ A class set of calculators

Oral and mental starter

Objective: Recall facts in x2, x3, x4, x5, x6, x10 tables.

○ Tell the children they are to 'test' each other's times tables. They should work in pairs with one calculator between them. The first child enters + 2 =. The second child has to say what comes next in the 2 x table. (With some calculators you have to key in 2 + + =.) The first child presses the equals key and tells the second child if they were correct or not. Give children the appropriate times table to practise.

Problem-solving challenge

What can you do with number 4?

With the whole class

○ Write on the board +, −, x, ÷, = and the number 4. Explain that today's challenge is to see if they can get as answers all the numbers from 1 to 20 using only the number 4 and any operation. Tell them that the number 4 can be used as often as they like. It can be combined to make 44 or 444, if it helps! Ask if anyone can suggest how to get the number 8. It is best not to have too much whole-class discussion at this point but let the children discuss amongst themselves. Tell them they can use whichever calculation method they like: mental, pencil and paper or the calculator. Whichever method they choose, they should check their work by an appropriate method. Stress that you do not want to see them using the calculator for really easy calculations! Also emphasise the need to record the steps as they go along. Otherwise they will forget what they have entered into the calculator.

Children working individually/in pairs

○ Set the children off on their task.

○ The children will, very quickly, understand the problem, if not the answers! Stop the class and ask for answers to some of the numbers. The 'secret' to this investigation is 4 ÷ 4 = 1. Once they have realised that fact they can find the answers quite quickly.

Plenary

○ This will depend upon the challenges you have set the children but ask questions about them. For example, 'Who thinks they have found the shortest way?' Write some of the children's ways on the board.

○ Ask the children how they checked their work. What strategies did they use?

Development

○ There are many ways to develop this activity. Here are some suggestions:

- What is the shortest way to find each number?
- What is the longest way to find each number?
- What answers can you find if you are only allowed to use each operation once?
- What answers can you find if you are only allowed to use the 4 four times?

Support

○ To make the problem more open ended, tell the children they have to find any numbers they can. They will find this easier than trying to find specific numbers.

Extension

○ Many of the challenges listed in 'Development' would be appropriate for extending more able children.

○ Another way would be to set the children target numbers, such as 256, 176, 88, 26 and –8, and see if they can work out how to get to those numbers.

Some answers to those are:
$256 = 4 \times 4 \times 4 \times 4$
$176 = 44 + 44 + 44 + 44$, or 44×4, or $4 \div 4 \times 4 \times 44$
$88 = 44 + 44$
$26 = 44 + 44 \div 4 + 4$
$-8 = 4 - 4 - 4 - 4$

○ The children could make up target number challenges for each other.

Questions to guide assessment

○ Did the children use appropriate calculation methods?
○ Did the children tackle the problems in a logical way?
○ Did the children use appropriate checking strategies?

Max Factor!

Framework for Numeracy objectives

Solving problems

○ Solve mathematical problems or puzzles, recognise and explain patterns and relationships, generalise and predict. Suggest extensions asking 'What if...?'

Calculations

○ Find all the pairs of factors of any number up to 100.
○ Develop calculator skills and use a calculator effectively.
○ Use the relationship between multiplication and division.

VOCABULARY

factors

Resources

○ Calculators
○ OHP calculator
○ Multiplication squares
○ Photocopiable Sheets 14 and 15 (pages 55 and 56)

Oral and mental starter

Objective: Find pairs with the sum of 100.

○ Play the 'Make me 100' game. The children play in pairs (equal in ability) with one calculator between two. The first child has to enter a TU number and hand the calculator to their partner. The second child has to add to that number to make 100 on the calculator. If they get a correct answer they win a point. The first child to 10 points wins. It would be appropriate for less able children to be allowed to use jottings, number lines or a hundred square to help them.

Problem-solving challenge

Which number has the most factors?

With the whole class

○ Tell the children what a 'factor' is – any number that can divide exactly into another. Demonstrate on the board how to find the factors of a number such as 36. Ask the children questions such as:

• How could we find the factors of this number?
• What strategies could we use?
• How could we use what we know about multiplication and division to help us?
• How will we know when we have got all the factors?

○ Ask the children to work either mentally or with a calculator to find as many factors as they can. If you have an OHP calculator they could come out to the front and use that. If they are unsure repeat the above using another number.

○ Tell the children that today's challenge is to find the number between 1 and 100 that has the most factors. Ask them what number they think it could be and why. Ask them if anyone thinks there will be a few numbers with the same number of factors.

Children working as individuals/pairs/groups

Organisation of this activity can be in various ways:

a) The children all tackle the problem either individually or in pairs.
b) The class is divided into various groups and each group tries to find the factors of a range of numbers, for example 1 to 20 or 20 to 40.

Plenary

○ Ask the children to say which of their numbers had the most factors. Take responses from a few children. Ask them to write the number and factor on the board. Ask the rest of the class to check if it is correct and that there are no factors missing. If no child has the correct answer (48) tell them that they could try and find it out at home.

Support

○ Limit the numbers the children have to find the factors of. For example, they only have to find the factors of all the numbers up to 20.

○ Let the children use photocopiable Sheets 14 and/or 15 (pages 55 and 56) to help them.

○ The children would also benefit from having access to a multiplication square, which could help them find the factors.

Extension

○ Can these children find the number between 50 and 100 that has the most factors?

○ Ask 'Do all the square numbers below 100 have an odd number of factors?'

Questions to guide assessment

○ Did the children tackle the problem in a systematic way?
○ Did the children use their knowledge of inverses to help solve the problem?
○ Did the children use the calculator appropriately?

Multiplication triangles

Framework for Numeracy objectives

Solving problems

○ Solve mathematical problems or puzzles, recognise and explain patterns and relationships, generalise and predict. Suggest extensions asking 'What if...?'

Calculations

○ Know by heart all multiplication facts up to 10 x 10.
○ Use informal pencil and paper methods to support, record or explain additions.
○ Find all the pairs of factors of any number up to 100.
○ Check with an equivalent calculation.

> **VOCABULARY**
>
> equivalent

Resources

○ Photocopiable Sheets 16 and 17 (pages 57 and 58)
○ A multiplication table square

Oral and mental starter

Objective: Order positive and negative whole numbers.

○ Ask five children for a two-digit number. Write the numbers on the board. Then ask five children for five negative two-digit numbers. Tell the class they have x minutes to write the ten numbers in order, starting from the lowest negative number. Repeat this.

Problem-solving challenge

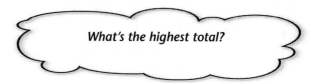

What's the highest total?

With the whole class

○ Draw the following triangle on the board.

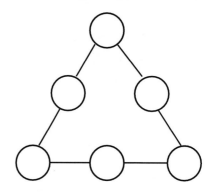

○ Explain to the children that you have to put the digits 1–6 into the circles and then multiply the numbers on each side. When you have done that you add the side totals. Like this:

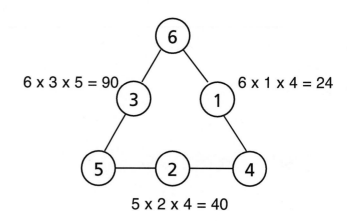

$6 \times 3 \times 5 = 90$

$6 \times 1 \times 4 = 24$

$5 \times 2 \times 4 = 40$

$90 + 40 + 24 = 154$

Children working as individuals/pairs

○ Explain that today's challenge is to find the highest and lowest totals possible using the triangle. Give the children copies of photocopiable Sheet 16 (page 57). Tell them that they have to record on the sheet in the same way that you did on the board. But they have to put the numbers 1 to 6 in a different order, aiming to make the lowest possible total and the highest possible total. Talk to them about checking. Say that you are expecting them to check by doing an equivalent calculation. In this instance by checking both the multiplication and addition by starting from a different number. Stress to the children the fact that with addition and multiplication, it does not matter in which order you add or multiply the numbers.

○ The solutions to the highest and lowest are:

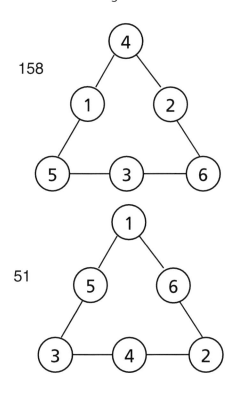

○ When they have found the highest and lowest ask them to try and find as many other totals as they can.

○ When they have investigated other totals give them photocopiable Sheet 17 (page 58). Ask them to write down some of their line totals and then to try and find all the factors for each number.

Plenary

○ Ask the children to tell you what strategies they used to find the totals. Draw on the board the solution to the highest total and then a blank triangle next to it. Ask the children where they would put 7, 8, 9, 10, 11 and 12 in this triangle to get the highest total. Let them discuss this in pairs. Hopefully they will follow the pattern of the original solution (the highest numbers in the corners).

○ Ask the children to tell you about their checking strategies.

Support

○ Rather than asking the children to multiply mentally let them use either informal written methods or a multiplication table square to help them.

Extension

○ Ask the children to try and find three different solutions to one total. For example:

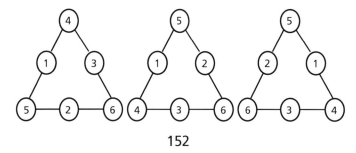

152

○ Another extension activity could be to investigate six other consecutive numbers. If they were to choose numbers like 21, 22, 23, 24, 25 and 26 it could be quite challenging, without a calculator!

Questions to guide assessment

○ Could the children multiply the numbers accurately?
○ Did the children check their calculations?
○ Could the children extend the problem by asking questions like, 'What if...?'

The missing digits!

Framework for Numeracy objectives

Solving problems
- Solve mathematical problems or puzzles, recognise and explain patterns and relationships, generalise and predict. Suggest extensions asking 'What if...?'

Calculations
- Know by heart all multiplication facts up to 10 x 10.
- Use the relationship between multiplication and division.
- Develop calculator skills and use a calculator effectively.
- Check with the inverse operation when using a calculator.

VOCABULARY

inverse, multiplication, division

Resources
- Photocopiable Sheets 18 to 20 (pages 59 to 61)
- An OHP calculator
- Individual calculators

Oral and mental starter

Objective: Begin to recall facts in x7, x8 and x9 tables and squares to 10 x 10.

- Give the children photocopiable Sheet 18 (page 59). Ask them to put a cross on all the numbers that are in the 7, 8 and 9 times tables as quickly as possible. Alternatively, you could say 'Put a cross on all the multiples of 7, 8 and 9.'

- Tell the children to put circles around the answers to 2 x 2, 3 x 3 and so on up to 10 x 10.

- Ask what these special numbers are called.

Problem-solving challenge

Which digits are missing?

With the whole class

- The children should have calculators.

- Write on the board ☐ x ☐ x ☐ = 140. Ask the children how they think they could solve this puzzle. Tell them that each ☐ is a single digit number. Their first response, no doubt, will be to say that you choose three digits and try them. Let them work with a partner to see if they can solve the challenge by this 'trial and error' method. Some of them may get a correct answer; if so write it on the board. (Possible answers are: 7 x 4 x 5 or 4 x 7 x 5.)

- Tell the children that there may be another solution to this problem and ask them to see if they can find it. Let them try for a while before stopping them. Ask if anyone can think of a more systematic way of doing this. Explain that a better way would involve using the inverse of multiplication. Ask what that is. Ask the children if anyone could think of a way of finding the answers using division. Explain that you divide the target number by a single digit. If the answer is a whole number you can divide it again. This will give you the three single-digit numbers you need. (140 ÷ 5 = 28. 28 ÷ 7 = 4. You have the numbers 5, 7 and 4. 5 x 7 x 4 is the other solution to the problem.) Demonstrate this on the OHP calculator. Also demonstrate how some divisions will give you a decimal and therefore are incorrect. Once you have got the three numbers demonstrate how to check by actually multiplying the numbers. Do the children think that the order in which you multiply the numbers matters?

Children working individually

○ Give the children photocopiable Sheet 19 (page 60) to complete.

Plenary

○ Ask the children if anyone thought of a logical way to complete the activity sheet. The most sensible way would be to divide the number by 9 first, then 8 first and so on.

○ Ask the children how their knowledge of multiplication tables helped in solving the problem.

○ Write on the board ?? x ?1 = 1281 (61 x 21). Ask the children to give you the solution.

Support

○ Give the children photocopiable Sheet 20 (page 61) to complete. This has some of the single digits already entered.

Extension

○ Let the children make up number puzzles like this for each other to try. The number of boxes allowed can be increased, to say four or even five.

Questions to guide assessment

○ Did the children adopt a methodical approach to solving the problems?
○ Did the children use the calculator appropriately both to calculate and to check?
○ Did the children use their multiplication tables or did they rely on the calculator?

A prime example!

Framework for Numeracy objectives

Solving problems

○ Choose and use appropriate number operations to solve problems, and appropriate ways of calculating: mental, mental with jottings, written methods and using the calculator.

Measures, shape and space

○ Approximate first. Use informal pencil and paper methods to support, record or explain multiplications and divisions.
○ Develop calculator skills and use a calculator effectively.
○ Check with the inverse operation when using a calculator.
○ Recognise prime numbers to at least 19.

> ### VOCABULARY
> angle, corner, edge, side, straight, triangle

Resources

○ Calculators
○ Photocopiable Sheets 21 and 22 (pages 62 and 63)

Oral and mental starter

Objective: Give pairs of factors up to 100.

○ Split the class into pairs of children. Give each pair a calculator. One child has to say a number between 1 and 100, the other child has to say two factors of that number. The first child, if not certain can check with a calculator. Challenge the children to think of factors other than the number itself and 1. Unless, of course, it is a prime number, which will be a nice lead in to the main part of the lesson.

Problem-solving challenge

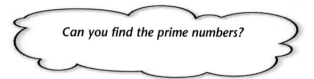

Can you find the prime numbers?

> ### With the whole class

○ Write the number 20 on the board and ask the children to tell you all the numbers that will divide into 20 exactly. As they say the numbers, write them on the board. (20,1, 5, 4, 10, 2)

○ Now write the number 19 on the board and ask the children to tell you all the numbers that will divide exactly into 19. Explain that any number that can only be divided by itself and 1 is called a 'prime number'. The Ancient Greek philosopher Euclid is generally acknowledged to have discovered prime numbers. He lived from 330–275BC. Perhaps some discussion of the concept of BC would be in order at this point!

○ Tell the children to work quietly with a partner for a few minutes to find all the prime numbers from 1 to 20. They can use any calculation method they feel is appropriate. Ask them to check their calculations by an appropriate method.

○ Give them enough time to find all the prime numbers but don't worry if not every pair has finished. Ask the children for all the numbers they think are prime and write them on the board. (2, 3, 5, 7, 11, 13, 17, 19). Ask them which method of calculation they used and how they checked the answers were correct.

○ Now ask them if they think that the number 1 is a prime number. Ask them to vote on it and defend their decision! Remind them that the rule for being a prime number is that it can only be divided by itself and 1. Since itself is 1 it cannot be divided by two different numbers; therefore 1 is not a prime number.

○ Ask the children what they think would happen if they divided one prime number by another prime number? Do they think the answer will always be a decimal? Let them investigate this, using calculators.

○ Take feedback from the children and correct any misconceptions.

Children working individually

○ Give the children photocopiable Sheet 21 (page 62). Explain that they have to find which prime number has been divided by which prime number to give the answers in each box. They can use whichever method of calculation they like but they must write down how they checked the answer.

Answers
1) $3.8 = 19 \div 5$
2) $8.5 = 17 \div 2$
3) $6.5 = 13 \div 2$
4) $1.5714285 = 11 \div 7$
5) $4.3333333 = 13 \div 3$
6) $6.3333333 = 19 \div 3$
7) $1.4 = 7 \div 5$
8) $0.4117647 = 7 \div 17$
9) $0.1052631 = 2 \div 19$
10) $0.2941176 = 5 \div 17$

Plenary

○ Discuss the activities on the sheets with the children. Ask them what methods they used to check their answers.

○ Ask them to tell you what a prime number is.

○ You might like to finish the lesson by telling them that in 1992 a computer discovered a prime number that was so big it had 227,832 digits in it!

Support

○ With the initial investigation, let the children use calculators and encourage them to adopt a logical approach to finding the prime numbers.

○ Let these children do photocopiable Sheet 22 (page 63). This gives them one of the two numbers they need to find for each challenge.

Extension

○ Let the children investigate other prime numbers. They could find all the prime numbers from 2 to 100 or beyond if it is appropriate.

○ Ask them to investigate this question: 'Can every number greater than 2 be written as the sum of two prime numbers?'

Questions to guide assessment

○ Did the children use the calculators appropriately?
○ Did the children adopt a systematic approach to solving the problems?
○ Did the children use appropriate checking strategies?

Test those numbers!

Framework for Numeracy objectives

Solving problems

○ Choose and use appropriate number operations to solve problems, and appropriate ways of calculating: mental, mental with jottings, written methods and using the calculator.

○ Make and investigate a general statement about familiar numbers or shapes by finding examples that satisfy it.

Calculations

○ Know and apply tests of divisibility by 2, 4, 5, 10 or 100.

○ Develop calculator skills and use a calculator effectively.

○ Check with the inverse operation when using a calculator.

> ### VOCABULARY
> multiple, tests of divisibility, divisible, sum

Resources

○ Number fans
○ Calculators
○ Photocopiable Sheets 23 to 25 (pages 64 to 66)

Oral and mental starter

Objective: Multiply mentally any two-digit number by a one-digit number.

○ Give the children a range of 'quick fire' questions. For example, 18 x 2, 15 x 4 and so on. They should use their number fans to show you the answers. Tell them that as soon as they have worked out the answer they should hold the number fans to their chest until you say 'David Beckham' (or another popular figure)! After each question, ask them which strategy they used to work out the answer.

Problem-solving challenge

> *Can we find a quick way to divide numbers?*

With the whole class

○ Either enlarge photocopiable Sheet 23 (page 64) and display it or give the children their own copies of it. Work through each statement in turn with the following activities. Try to keep the class working together as much as possible.

1) A number can be divided exactly by 10, if the last digit is 0.

Ask the children to give you an example of a three-digit number that is divisible by 10. Write the number on the board. Ask them how they could check the answer is correct. There will be a range of responses, no doubt! Ask who would check it by doing a mental division calculation; by a mental calculation using jottings; by pencil and paper methods or by using a calculator. Ask various children how they would do it in their chosen way. (It is to be hoped that most children would do the division calculation mentally!) Ask them how they would check that their answer was correct. Stress that checking by the inverse is a very efficient method in this case.

With the children working in pairs, ask them to write down a four-digit number and tell their partner how they would check whether it is divisible by 10.

2) A number can be divided exactly by 2, if the last digit is 0, 2, 4, 6 or 8.

Ask a child to tell you a three-digit number that ends in an even number. Ask the others how we could check that it is divisible by 2. Hopefully they will say that the obvious way to do this is to halve the number mentally.

With the children working in pairs again, tell them that one child has to say a four-digit even number and the other child has to halve that number as quickly as possible. Then they take turns to do this for a short while.

3) A number can be divided exactly by 3, if the sum of the digits is divisible by 3.

Ask a child for a three-digit number and test the statement to see if it is correct. Try this with a couple more three-digit numbers. Tell the children the activity is to find 10 four-digit numbers that divide by three exactly. They can record their answers on photocopiable Sheet 24 (page 65). They must show how they checked them either in numbers or in words.

4) A number can be divided exactly by 4, if the last two digits are divisible by 4.

Ask the children for a range of three-digit numbers and write them on the board. Test out the numbers on the board to see if they are divisible by 4. If not, ask the children if anyone can think of a number that would be divisible by 4 and try that one.

Tell them that they have some time to work with their partner to write down as many combinations of two digits that are divisible by 4 as they can. They can write their answers on photocopiable Sheet 24. Hopefully they will tackle this in a logical way – 12, 16, 20 and so on – rather than 'going at it' randomly!

5) A number can be divided exactly by 5, if the last digit is a five or a zero.

Ask the children to tell you a three-digit number and write it on the board. Use the test of divisibility to see if it will divide by five. Repeat this for a few numbers.

6) A number can be divided exactly by 6, if the number is even and divisible by 3.

Tell the children they have to work in pairs to find as many four-digit numbers as they can that divide by 6 exactly. They can record their answers on Sheet 25.

7) A number can be divided exactly by 8, if the last three digits can be divided by 8.

Ask the children to talk to each other about three-digit numbers that can be divided by 8 exactly. Ask them to think of a way of finding the answers by using the inverse of division (such as 16 x 24). Let them use calculators and find as many as they can.

They can record their answers on Sheet 25. Ask the children for some of their answers and write them on the board. Ask the pairs of children to think of six-digit numbers that can be divided by eight. Hopefully the children will realise that they can put any digits in front of their three-digit answers!

8) A number can be divided by 9, if the sum of the digits is divisible by 9.

Investigate this statement with the whole class as a mental maths activity. Ask the children to think of three digits that add up to 9, such as 5 + 3 + 1. Ask them what three-digit numbers could be made from these digits. Extend this to asking the children to think of three digits that add up to 18.

Plenary

○ Write the number 240 on the board. Ask the children to use their tests of divisibility to work out what numbers will divide into it exactly. (2, 3, 4, 5, 6, 10)

○ Ask them to think of other three-digit numbers that have a wide range of factors. Write some of them on the board and discuss them with the class.

Support

○ Depending on the ability of the children, just let them investigate a few of the simpler statements.

Extension

○ Challenge the children to do as much of this work as possible mentally and on REALLY BIG numbers

Questions to guide assessment

○ Could the children apply the tests of divisibility accurately?
○ Did the children use appropriate checking strategies?
○ Did the children cooperate and discuss the problems?

Let's build a fence!

Framework for Numeracy objectives

Solving problems

○ Identify and use appropriate operations (including combinations of operations) to solve word problems involving numbers and quantities based on 'real life', money or measures, using one or more steps.

○ Choose and use appropriate number operations to solve problems, and appropriate ways of calculating: mental, mental with jottings, written methods and using the calculator.

Shape and space

○ Calculate the perimeter and area of simple compound shapes that can be split into rectangles.

Calculations

○ Develop calculator skills and use a calculator effectively.

VOCABULARY

area, perimeter

Resources

○ Squared paper
○ Calculators

Oral and mental starter

Objective: Derive sums and differences, for example 760 ± 280.

○ Split the class into pairs. Write two three-digit numbers on the board. One of each pair has to calculate the sum and write it down; the other has to calculate the difference and write that down. The children swop answers and check each other's answers. Ask them how they calculated the answers. Repeat this a few times.

Problem-solving challenge

What's the cheapest fencing?

With the whole class

○ Explain that today's challenge involves Farmer Growitall! Farmer Growitall has been asked by the government to grow a new type of crop. This is a very special crop so it must be protected from any animals that might eat it. Therefore the field will have to have a fence around it. The government only wants a small amount of this crop grown.

○ For the first challenge, the government wants 12 square metres of crop grown. Farmer Growitall wants to find the cheapest and the dearest ways to build a fence around the 12 square metres. To make it easier to plant the crop he wants it to be grown in a rectangular shape. Fencing costs £25 per metre.

○ Ask the children to discuss, in pairs, how they might try to solve this problem. Stress that you do not want the answers at this stage. Take feedback from the children. Depending on their response, explain that this is a problem involving area and perimeter. You may need to remind them what these concepts are.

Children working individually/in pairs

○ Give the children some squared paper and ask them to investigate the various costs involved. Resist the temptation to give them more guidance at this stage. They have to learn how to interpret a problem and make sense of it by themselves.

○ Stop the children after a short while and ask them to explain to you some of their findings. Ask them what methods of calculation they are using and how they are checking their work. Ask what were the cheapest and the dearest costs they found.
(Answers: 12 x 1 = £650, 6 x 2 = £400, 3 x 4 = £350)

○ The lesson can now be developed in a number of ways, all based on the fact that you have received a phone call from the farmer! Choose from the following:

- The farmer has decided that he does not have to plant in a rectangular shape. It can be any shape that has an area of 12 square metres.

- The farmer has rung to say that the fencing has been increased (or decreased) in price to x amount. The amount will depend on how successfully the children have tackled the first problem.

- The farmer has had a phone call from the government to say that they have increased (or decreased) the amount of square metres they need to be grown.

- The farmer has received a phone call from the government to say they want two plots of crops grown. One 10 square metres and the other 14 square metres.

Plenary

○ Ask the children to explain how they solved the problem you set them. Concentrate on the strategies they used to solve the problem and the methods of calculation they used.

○ Explain that although this was a made-up problem, the cost of fencing is a very real one. Ask the children if they can think of places in the school neighbourhood that need a fence and what shape these places are.

Support

○ Rather than get the children to solve the problem of 12 square metres, give them an area within their ability range. It may be appropriate to just ask them to calculate the perimeter and not worry about the cost element.

Extension

○ Use the bullet pointed scenarios to extend the more able. Obviously choose areas and costs that will stretch their ability.

Questions to guide assessment

○ Did the children have efficient strategies to solve the problems?
○ Did the children choose appropriate methods of calculation?
○ Could they calculate area and perimeter easily?

Triangle sum

Framework for Numeracy objectives

Solving problems
○ Choose and use appropriate number operations to solve problems, and appropriate ways of calculating: mental, mental with jottings, written methods and using the calculator.
○ Make and investigate a general statement about familiar shapes by finding examples that satisfy it.

Shape and space
○ Use a protractor to measure and draw acute and obtuse angles to the nearest degree.
○ Check that the sum of the angles of a triangle is 180°: for example, by measuring or paper folding.

VOCABULARY

angle, isosceles, scalene, equilateral, right-angled

Resources
○ Whiteboards
○ Protractors
○ Rulers
○ Photocopiable Sheets 26 and 27 (pages 67 and 68)

Oral and mental starter

Objective: To order fractions.

○ Ask some of the children to tell you some fractions – around five to start with. Write the fractions on the board randomly. Ask the children to put them in order as quickly as they can, starting from the smallest. They can record on whiteboards or paper. Discuss their answers with the children and talk about how we can order fractions.

Problem-solving challenge

Does the sum of all the angles of a triangle equal 180˚?

With the whole class

○ Draw a semicircle on the board. Ask the children if they think that it is possible to draw a triangle within the semicircle. Invite someone out to the front to draw a triangle in the semicircle. Ask the class what type of triangle it is. Repeat this with other children, asking again what type of triangles have been drawn. If certain types of triangles haven't been drawn, challenge the children to come out and draw an equilateral triangle, for example.

○ Now tell the children you are going to set them a challenge. Ask whether if you draw a straight line along the bottom of the semicircle and see that this is the bottom side of a triangle, any triangle that you draw that touches the side of the semicircle will be right-angled. Demonstrate this on the board.

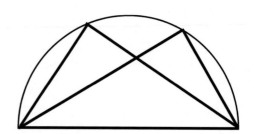

Children working individually/in pairs

○ Give the children protractors, rulers and copies of photocopiable Sheet 26 (page 67). Ask them to investigate this challenge. For each triangle they draw they must put in the measurements of each angle and write the sum of the angles.

○ After a while, ask the children to listen for a moment before you give them another challenge. Ask them if the answer to the question is 'Yes'. (It is!) Now ask them for the total measurements of all the angles in a triangle.

○ Now give the children photocopiable Sheet 27 (page 68). Tell the children the challenge this time is to draw a triangle in each circle but to draw as many different types of triangle as they can. For each triangle they should write in the size of the angles and the sum of the angles.

Plenary

○ Remind the children of the properties of different types of triangle. Ask them to show you an example of each type of triangle and tell you the properties of the triangle.

○ Ask the children to tell you what they have found out about the sum of the angles of a triangle. Draw a large and a small triangle on the board and ask the children for the sum of the angles in each one.

Support

○ It would be better just to let these children do the second challenge of drawing triangles in circles. The emphasis should be on measuring the drawn angles accurately. If it is appropriate, ask them to add up the angles in each triangle they have drawn.

Extension

○ Ask these children to cut out some of the triangles they have drawn and investigate combinations of angles by combining triangles.

Questions to guide assessment

○ Could the children draw and measure the angles correctly?
○ Did the children remember the names and properties of triangles?
○ Could the children generalise about the sum of the angles in a triangle?

Time machine

Framework for Numeracy objectives

Solving problems
- Identify and use appropriate operations (including combinations of operations) to solve word problems involving numbers and quantities based on 'real life' or measures (including time), using one or more steps.
- Explain methods and reasoning.

Calculations
- Appreciate different times around the world.

VOCABULARY

time zones, a.m., p.m.

Resources
- Photocopiable Sheets 28 to 32 (pages 69 to 73)
- A large world map or atlases (optional)

Oral and mental starter

Objective: Add/subtract any pair of two-digit numbers including crossing 100.

- Write on the board a number between 100 and 150. Ask the children to think of two numbers that will add together to equal that number. As soon as they have thought of an answer they should put their hands on their heads! There will of course be lots of different answers. Ask a few children for their answers. Repeat this a few times.

- Write a number below 50 on the board. This time the children have to think of two numbers that, when the smaller is subtracted from the larger, equal the target number. When they know the answers, they have to put a finger on their nose! Repeat this a few times.

Problem-solving challenge

Can you find the times around the world?

With the whole class

- Explain to the children that the time is different in different places around the world. For example, if it was 09.17 in London it would be 04.17 in New York. Write those times on the board as 24 hour clock times. Ask the children what time of day it would be in New York. Would it be am or pm? Ask them why they think we have different times. If no-one in the class knows, explain it to them.

- Display an enlarged copy of photocopiable Sheet 28 (page 69) and give the children their own copies. Ask different children to read out the place names on the sheet and after each one ask if anyone knows which country each city is in. (If you want to extend the lesson into geography, have a large world map or atlases and let the children find each city.) Then, once you have found each place, read out the time alongside it on the sheet and ask the children to convert these 24 hour clock times to 12 hour clock times, and say whether they are am or pm.

- Explain how to calculate the difference by counting on or back and give the children one or two to do. Encourage them to do the calculations mentally but say that on their own copies of the sheet they can put any jottings in the box at the bottom.

Children working in pairs

○ Explain that Professor Fruitcake has invented a very fast aeroplane! It has made flights all around the world a lot quicker. For example, you can now fly to New York in $2\frac{1}{2}$ hours. Give the children this problem. 'If you left London airport at 09.17, what would be the time in New York when you landed?' Ask the children to discuss how to work out the answer. (06.47)

○ Ask the children which method they used to solve the problem. You can challenge their thinking by saying that you would have landed before you took off!

○ Now ask the children what the time would be in New York when the plane landed if the plane left London at 10.05. (07.35) Ask them to explain their methods.

○ Give the children photocopiable Sheet 29 (page 70). Explain that you want all the answers recorded in the 24 hour clock way. They could not be expected to do all the calculations mentally, so give them photocopiable Sheet 30 (page 71) to record how they did each question.

Answers

1) 7.47	2) 10.47	3) 16.47
4) 20.57	5) 21.57	6) 23.57
7) 15.17	8) 16.59	9) 20.30
10) 06.29	11) 08.29	12) 11.42
13) 22.02	14) 02.02	15) 06.02

Plenary

○ Take feedback from the children about the methods they used to answer the questions. Ask them if they found any shortcuts or quicker ways to answer some of the questions.

○ Ask if any of the children have heard about 'jet-lag'? Talk to them about it because it is a good example of mathematics in the real world.

Support

○ For the 'find the difference' problem let the children answer in hours. For the second activity give them photocopiable Sheet 31 (page 72). This has easier flight times for them to calculate.

Answers

1) 7.17	2) 10.17	3) 16.17
4) 18.17	5) 19.17	6) 21.17
7) 16.17	8) 17.17	9) 21.17
10) 06.17	11) 08.17	12) 11.17

Extension

○ Ask the children to make up their own questions for each other or you (!) to answer. A blank template is on photocopiable Sheet 32 (page 73). This can be used for the children to write their own times and flight times.

Questions to guide assessment

○ Could the children cope with the time calculations?
○ Did they persevere with the work?
○ Did they calculate with efficient methods?

Number polygons

Framework for Numeracy objectives

Solving problems
○ Solve mathematical problems or puzzles, recognise and explain patterns and relationships, generalise and predict. Suggest extensions asking 'What if...?'
○ Choose and use appropriate number operations to solve problems, and appropriate ways of calculating: mental, mental with jottings, written methods, calculator.

Calculations
○ Develop calculator skills and use a calculator effectively.
○ Use informal pencil and paper methods to support, record or explain additions and subtractions.
○ Use informal pencil and paper methods to support, record or explain multiplications and divisions.

> **VOCABULARY**
>
> multiplication, division, negative numbers, decimals

Resources
○ Number cards 1 to 100
○ Calculators
○ Photocopiable Sheets 33 and 34 (pages 74 and 75)

Oral and mental starter

Objective: Recall multiplication and division facts to 10 x 10.

○ Using a set of 1 to 100 number cards, give each child a couple of cards. Explain that you are going to ask a question such as 'What is a multiple of 8?' The first child to stand up with a number that is a multiple of 8 wins. Ask other questions such as 'What is a number that can be divided by 5?'

Problem-solving challenge

> *What are the highest and lowest totals?*

With the whole class

○ Draw a large polygon on the board with circles in it like the one below and write the numbers 1 to 10 in the circles randomly.

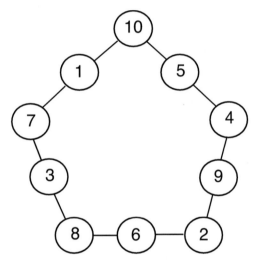

8 x 6 x 2 = 96

○ Tell the children they have to multiply the numbers in the circles on each side of the shape and then add those totals. So, when multiplied, the three numbers on the horizontal side of the shape in the example above total 96. Do the same for the other sides of the polygon. Demonstrate this on the board asking the children to help you with the multiplications. Although they can use the calculator for this challenge, encourage them to use their mental skills to make the calculations more efficient. For example, when multiplying 8, 6 and 2, it is easiest to do 6 x 2 = 12, x 8 = 96.

○ Explain that the first part of the challenge today is to try and find the highest and lowest totals they can.

Children working individually/in pairs

○ Give the children copies of photocopiable Sheet 33 (page 74) on which to record their calculations. Don't give them any more guidance at this stage; let them explore the problem for themselves. If they have done other similar problems from this series of books they may realise straight away that, to get the highest possible total, the highest numbers go in the corners because they are used twice. The next highest number is put between the two highest corner numbers and so on. Conversely for the lowest total the lowest numbers go in the corners.

○ If the children are finding it difficult give them a few 'clues', like; 'If I were you I would put the 10 in the top circle!'

Answers

The solutions to the highest and lowest are:

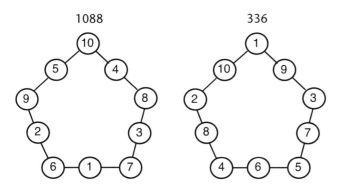

1088   336

○ When the children have found the highest and lowest give them a copy of photocopiable Sheet 34 (page 75) and tell them to choose one of the polygons to investigate the numbers. Tell them they have to choose a start number and then write the numbers down in order, going in either direction on the sheet (forwards or backwards). They then have to either subtract or divide the numbers to find a total. In the first instance suggest they do only one operation at a time with the numbers. Here are some examples of what can happen:

$10 - 2 - 9 - 4 - 6 - 1 - 7 - 5 - 8 - 3 = -35$
$6 - 1 - 7 - 5 - 8 - 3 - 10 - 2 - 9 - 4 = -43$

$10 \div 2 \div 9 \div 4 \div 6 \div 1 \div 7 \div 5 \div 8 \div 3 = 0.0000275$
$6 \div 1 \div 7 \div 5 \div 8 \div 3 \div 10 \div 2 \div 9 \div 4 = 0.0000099$

○ Encourage the children to think of their own challenges starting from different numbers. For example, when subtracting, what start number will give the lowest negative number? Or when dividing, what start number will give the lowest decimal number?

○ Challenge them to pose 'What if...?' type questions, such as 'What if I use division once, then subtraction, then division and so on?' and 'What if I use multiplication and addition?'

Plenary

○ Talk to the children about the pentagon problem and the strategies they used to try and solve it.

○ Talk to the children about their number chains. Ask them who came up with some interesting results. Ask the children to describe what they found out.

Support

○ For the polygon activity it would be appropriate to get the children to add the sides of the polygons rather than multiply them. They can then investigate the addition totals, highest and lowest.

Extension

○ Ask the children to investigate other series of consecutive numbers and see if they can transfer the strategies from this problem to another.

○ Ask the children to 'invent' other shape challenges involving octagons, for example.

Questions to guide assessment

○ Did the children use the appropriate calculation method?
○ Did the children use the calculator appropriately?
○ Could the children pose their own mathematical questions?

Down to one!

Framework for Numeracy objectives

Solving problems

○ Solve mathematical problems or puzzles, recognise and explain patterns and relationships, generalise and predict. Suggest extensions asking 'What if...?'

○ Choose and use appropriate number operations to solve problems, and appropriate ways of calculating: mental, mental with jottings, written methods, calculator.

Calculations

○ Recognise squares of numbers to at least 12 x 12.
○ Add several numbers.

VOCABULARY

square numbers

Resources

○ An OHP calculator

Oral and mental starter

Objective: Recall squares.

○ Using the OHP calculator, enter a square number and ask the children what will be in the display when you press the square root key. Do this randomly at first to challenge the children. Then build up the pattern of square numbers 1, 4 and so on up to 100 and then carry on to see if the children can follow the pattern (121, 144, 169, 196, 225).

Problem-solving challenge

How can we reduce a number down to 1?

With the whole class

○ Write the number 8 on the board. Explain that we are going to explore what we can do with square numbers. Ask what the square number of 8 is, and then write 64 on the board. Then ask for the square of 6 and the square of 4 (the two numbers in the answer) and write on the board 36 + 16 = 52. Next ask for the squares of 5 and 2 and write those on the board. If you keep this process going you will get this sequence:

$25 + 4 = 29; 4 + 81 = 85; 64 + 25 = 89; 64 + 81 = 145; 1 + 16 + 25 = 42; 16 + 4 = 20; 4 + 0 = 4; 16; 1 + 36 = 37; 9 + 49 = 58; 25 + 64 = 89$

You will end up in a loop!

○ Ask the children to investigate all the other numbers from 1 to 10. They can do this either individually or with a partner. Or you could ask groups to do a couple of numbers each.

○ The children will discover that of all the numbers, only 7 does not go into a loop. It stops at 1.

Children working in groups

○ Split the class into groups and allocate to the groups a range of numbers to investigate to see if they can find any that will go down to 1. The range of numbers will depend on the ability of the class but for example numbers below 50 or between 50 and 100. The children will need to talk and agree who is to investigate which numbers.

○ If the children do not discover a number ask them to investigate 23.

23: $4 + 9 = 13$; $1 + 9 = 10$; $1 + 0 = 1$

○ Ask the children to see if they can find other numbers now. Hopefully they will realise that the same digits can be used including with a zero. (32, 203, 230 and so on.)

Plenary

○ Discuss with the children the patterns they have found and what numbers they found that could be reduced to 1.

○ Explain to the children that these numbers have been known in the past as 'happy' numbers! Ask if they can think of any other names to call them!

Support

○ To enable the class to work together as much as possible allow the children to use a prepared list of square numbers. If they struggle with the addition aspect, give them a number line to help.

Extension

○ The nature of this lesson is such that the children should be encouraged to challenge themselves to explore either larger numbers or other areas of investigation, exploring the repeating numbers in loops for example.

Questions to guide assessment

○ Could the children investigate independently?
○ Did any children explore other avenues of investigation?
○ Did the children calculate mentally?

Down the wall!

Framework for Numeracy objectives

Solving problems

○ Solve mathematical problems or puzzles, recognise and explain patterns and relationships, generalise and predict. Suggest extensions asking 'What if…?'

○ Choose and use appropriate number operations to solve problems, and appropriate ways of calculating: mental, mental with jottings, written methods and using the calculator.

Calculations

○ Use informal pencil and paper methods to support, record or explain multiplications and divisions.

○ Use the relationship between multiplication and division.

○ Develop calculator skills and use a calculator effectively.

○ Check with the inverse operation when using a calculator.

VOCABULARY

multiplication, division, divisibility, multiples

Resources

○ Calculators

○ Photocopiable Sheets 23 (page 64) and 35 to 37 (pages 76 to 78)

Oral and mental starter

Objective: Multiply or divide whole numbers by 10, 100 and 1000.

○ Give the children copies of photocopiable Sheet 35 (page 76). Then give them numbers to put in the left-hand column. Set them a time limit to perform the necessary calculations. When they have finished let them check their answers with calculators. This will give them an opportunity to observe how the numbers move left and right.

Problem-solving challenge

Can you get to the bottom of the wall?

With the whole class

○ Draw a wall on the board like the one below.

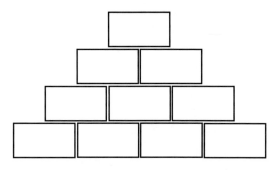

○ Write in the top brick 3456. Ask the children for two numbers that can be multiplied together to get this number. It is unlikely you will get a response apart, perhaps, for 2 x 1728! Give out copies of photocopiable Sheet 23 (page 64) 'Tests of divisibility'. Ask the children to look at the tests and see if that helps them solve the problem. Go through each test and see if it applies to the number.

1) ÷10? – No.

2) ÷2? – Yes.

3) ÷3? – The sum of its digits is 18 which is divisible by 3. (3 x 1152) Give the children calculators and ask them to see if the number can be divided by other multiples of 3. (3456 ÷ 6, 9, 12, 18, 24, and so on)

4) ÷4? – Yes.

5) ÷5? – No.

6) ÷6? – Yes. The number is even and divisible by 3. Ask the children to find other multiples of 6 that can divide into the number. Ask them if they are checking their divisions by the inverse operation.

7) ÷8? – Yes.

8) ÷9? – The sum of the digits is 18 which is divisible by 9. (9 x 384) Ask the children to find other multiples of 9 that will divide into the number.

Children working in pairs

○ Explain to the children that today's challenge is to fill the bricks with whole numbers. Give out copies of photocopiable Sheet 36 (page 77). Ask them to write 3456 in the top brick. Using some of the numbers they found using the tests of divisibility (or any other numbers that fit), they should put numbers in the next two bricks. Let them then investigate what three numbers will go into the row of three bricks. Tell them to use the tests of divisibility sheet and their calculators. Stress that you want to see them checking their answers by the inverse operation, so that, in theory, no-one should get anything incorrect!

○ Let the children 'have a go' at this for a while before stopping them and asking them what strategies they are using to get the answers. One very helpful strategy at this stage is to find the 'middle' brick first. Ask the children if they could do the divisions mentally, one would hope they could!

○ Finally, they have to find the bottom row of 'brick numbers'.

○ Ask if anyone has a bottom row that does not have 1 in it.

○ Let the children put another four-digit number in the top brick and then fill in the rest of the bricks, without putting 1 in any brick!

○ The children can use the calculator and/or mental calculations. They can work together but must check their calculations.

Plenary

○ Ask if any pairs of children found a wall that did not have 1 in it. Ask them to write the wall on the board and get the rest of the class to check the calculations.

○ Ask if the children used the tests of divisibility to help them or another strategy. Trial and error perhaps?

○ Finally thank the children for not driving you up the wall!

Support

○ Let the children start from the bottom bricks and multiply up but they must still check the wall by the inverse operation. They can either put any numbers they like in the bottom row or start with 1, 2, 3, 4 and see what the highest total is.

Extension

○ Give these children photocopiable Sheet 37 (page 78), which has larger brick walls so that the children can investigate larger numbers. For those doing this sheet, it is worth reminding them that if the calculator display shows E, it means error and the answer is wrong. This is likely to happen if the children try multiplying very big numbers. You could let them use the calculator that is on most computers. It allows you to perform bigger calculations. Alternatively talk with the children about partitioning the numbers so that you make the calculation easier.

Questions to guide assessment

○ Did the children use appropriate calculation strategies?
○ Did the children check by the inverse?
○ Did any child suggest an extension to the activity?

Where's the fire?

Framework for Numeracy objectives

Solving problems

○ Identify and use appropriate operations (including combinations of operations) to solve word problems involving numbers and quantities based on 'real life', money or measures (including time), using one or more steps.

Measures

○ Suggest suitable units and measuring equipment to estimate or measure length.

○ Use, read and write standard metric units (m, cm, mm).

VOCABULARY

metres, distance, centimetres

Resources

○ Stop watches
○ Measuring equipment
○ Photocopiable Sheet 38 (page 79)
○ Whiteboards

Oral and mental starter

Objective: To convert between km and mm.

○ Give the children 'quick fire' questions such as 'How many km are there is 2871mm?' and 'How many mm in 3km?'.

○ Ask them to respond by writing the answers on their whiteboards.

Problem-solving challenge

Can we find the quickest and safest fire escape route?

Note for the teacher

○ This lesson is very different from the others in this book because it relies very much on the layout of the school building. Therefore the lesson will need to be adapted to suit those local circumstances. In addition it may need to run over several days depending on the geography of the building and how many helpers you can use. It would be worth asking for parent volunteers to work with groups.

With the whole class

○ Start by talking to the children about the importance of fire drills and the need to behave sensibly during them. Ask the children to tell you where they should go in the event of a fire and what they should do. Tell them that to start with you are going to investigate times taken to evacuate various locations around the school. Some suggested locations are the classroom, the hall, the dining room and the computer suite. Select a child to use the stopwatch and time how long it takes for each fire drill.

○ When the children are back in school ask them to discuss ways in which the fire drill could be speeded up without the children rushing out of the building. Some of the suggestions will no doubt depend on the geography of the building but others may be more generic. For example, the way children line up; could that be speeded up? Perhaps a double line of children or children not lining up but just sensibly walking out of the building.

Children working in groups

○ No doubt the children will suggest alternative routes out of the building. These could be investigated by small groups of children. Split the class into groups to investigate the distances of various exit routes. Let them choose what measuring equipment they feel is most appropriate for the distance involved. They can also time how long it takes for each route. They can record their findings on photocopiable Sheet 38 (page 79).

○ Ask each group to report on their findings and say what their preferred exit route is and why.

○ Another area for investigation can be the exit routes taken by other classes. Groups of children can measure and time these and report on their findings.

○ Once these investigations have been carried out, consideration can be given to where the children assemble for the fire drill. Is this the 'best' location? Is it in a sufficiently safe place, away from a blazing building? What distance would be considered 'safe'? The children could decide upon a safe distance (30 metres?) and measure that distance out. Does the assembly point prevent access to the building by fire-fighters? If the assembly point is deemed not to be appropriate, where else could the school line up? If another point is chosen then there would be a need for groups to investigate the distances involved, as with the original point!

○ Groups of children could also investigate the distances involved in the exit routes of other members of the school community; office staff, kitchen staff, the caretaker, and so on.

Plenary

○ Gather together all the avenues of enquiry and split the class into groups to prepare a short presentation about what they have found out. Encourage the children to make positive suggestions about improving the fire drill. Perhaps the groups could present their findings to the rest of the school in an assembly.

Support and extension

○ If the children are put in mixed ability groups, they should be able to support each other. To create the climate of investigative work, encourage them to think of their own lines of enquiry.

Questions to guide assessment

○ Could the children work together in groups and cooperate?
○ Could the children think of their own lines of enquiry?
○ Could the children measure the distances accurately?

Name _____

The table below shows the distances in miles between towns.
Work out the cost of each journey for one person using
the following information. Then find the average costs.

Travel by car

If a car travels at 50mph, it will use one litre of petrol for
every 9 miles it travels. Petrol costs 81p per litre. Up to four
people can travel in this car.

Travel by taxi

To travel by taxi costs 20p per mile. Up to 5 people can travel in this taxi.

Travel by train

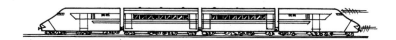

To travel by train costs 5p per mile for a single journey (one way) and 3p
per mile for a return journey. This price is per person.

Town	Town	Distance in miles	Car cost	Taxi cost	Train cost (single)
Abouttown	Bettertown	153			
Coldtown	Deartown	207			
Everytown	Fasttown	504			
Greattown	Hottown	801			
Idealtown	Jollytown	945			
		Totals			
		Average Costs			

Name _____

Record your calculations below.

A to B

Checked by:

C to D

Checked by:

E to F

Checked by:

G to H

Checked by:

I to J

Checked by:

Name _____

The table below shows the distances in miles between towns.
Work out the cost of each return journey (there and back again)
for a family of four using the following information.

Travel by car

If a car travels at 50mph it will use one litre of petrol
for every 9 miles it travels. Petrol costs 81p per litre.
Up to four people can travel in this car.

Travel by taxi

To travel by taxi costs £2.00 per mile. Up to five people can
travel in this taxi.

Travel by train

To travel by train costs 5p per mile for a single journey (one way) and 3p
per mile both ways if they make a return journey. This price is per person.

Town	Town	Distance in miles	Car cost	Taxi cost	Train cost
Abouttown	Bettertown	153			
Coldtown	Deartown	207			
Everytown	Fasttown	504			
Greattown	Hottown	801			
Idealtown	Jollytown	945			
		Totals			
		Average Costs			

Name _____

The table below shows the distances in miles between towns.
Work out the cost of each journey from one town to the other
for one person using the following information.

Travel by car

If a car travels at 50mph it will use one litre of petrol
for every 10 miles it travels. Petrol costs 80p per litre.

Travel by taxi

To travel by taxi costs £2.00 per mile.

Travel by train

To travel by train costs 5p per mile for a single journey.

Town	Town	Distance in miles	Car cost	Taxi cost	Train cost
Abouttown	Bettertown	10			
Coldtown	Deartown	20			
Everytown	Fasttown	30			
Greattown	Hottown	40			
Idealtown	Jollytown	50			
		Totals			

Name _____

The table below shows the distances between towns.
Work out the cost of each journey for one person using
the following information.

Travel by car

If a car travels at 50mph it will use one litre of petrol
for every _____ miles it travels. Petrol costs ___p per litre.
Up to four people can travel in this car.

Travel by taxi

To travel by taxi costs £_____ per mile. Up to five people can
travel in this taxi.

Travel by train

To travel by train costs ____p per mile for a single journey (one way)
and ____p per mile for both ways of a return journey. This price is per
person.

Town	Town	Distance in miles	Car cost	Taxi cost	Train cost
Abouttown	Bettertown	10			
Coldtown	Deartown	20			
Everytown	Fasttown	30			
Greattown	Hottown	40			
Idealtown	Jollytown	50			
		Totals			
		Average Costs			

Name _____

HOTEL SUNNY DELIGHT

SINGLE ROOM
Bed and breakfast price per night = €50

DOUBLE ROOM
Bed and breakfast price per night = €70

Deduct €5 per night Monday to Thursday

HOTEL HAPPY

Single room only price per night = €40

Double room only price per night = €60

Breakfast costs = €7

Deduct €4 per night Monday to Thursday

HOTEL GOODTIME

Single Room
bed and breakfast = €55 per night

Double Room
bed and breakfast = €75

Deduct €15 per night Monday to Thursday

Name _____

All rectangles...

have four right angles.

have opposite sides that are parallel and equal.

have diagonals that bisect each other.

have four lines of symmetry.

Choose one of the statements and write it here:

_____

_____

I agree/disagree with the statement because:

Name _____

All the sides are of equal length.

It has two sides of equal length.

All the sides are different lengths.

All the angles are equal.

Two of the angles are equal.

None of the angles is equal.

One of the angles is a right angle.

It has three lines of symmetry.

Isosceles

Scalene

Equilateral

Right angle

Name _____

Triangles

Name _____

Triangle descriptions

Sketch of triangle	Statement about the triangle

Name _____

Look at this plan. The routes shown are in kilometres.
Investigate the routes across from Start to Finish.

How many can you find? _____

What was your longest route? _____ km

What was your shortest route? _____ km

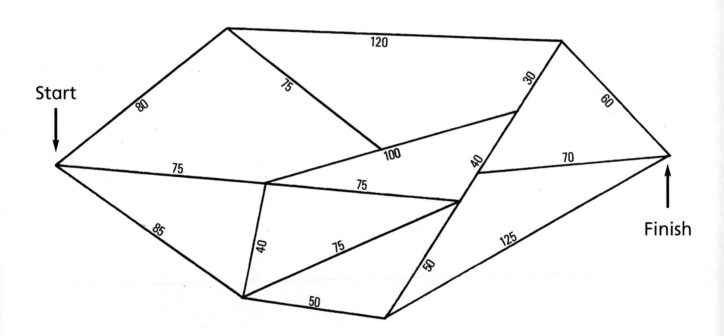

Name _____

Look at this plan. The routes shown are in kilometres.
Investigate the routes across from Start to Finish.

How many can you find? _____

What was your longest route? _____ km

What was your shortest route? _____ km

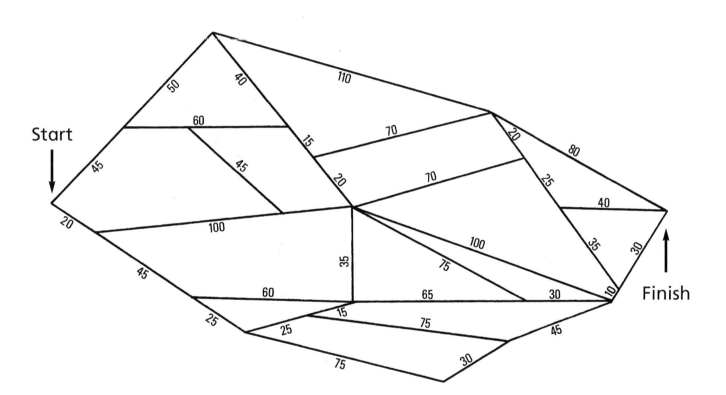

Name _____

Look at this plan. The routes shown are in kilometres.
Investigate the routes across from Start to Finish.

How many can you find? _____

What was your longest route? _____ km

What was your shortest route? _____ km

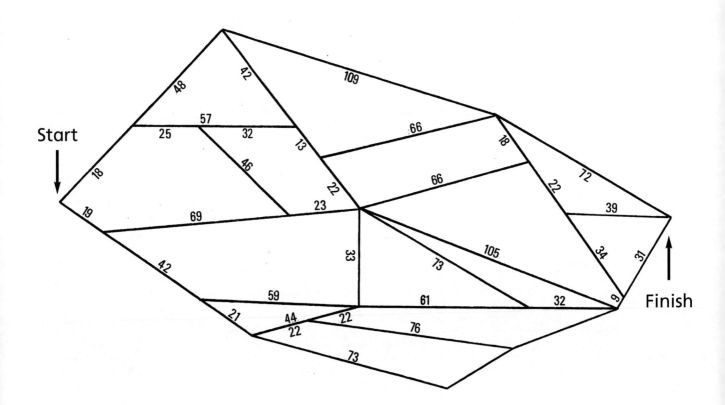

Name _____

Factors

Write the factors of the numbers around each one.
Some have been started for you.

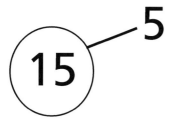

5

15

9

19

3

10

5

17

17

20

Name _____

Fill in the factors. Some have been started for you.

20	1							
21			7					
22								
23								
24				4				
25								
26								
27				27				
28		2						
29								

Find the factors of all the numbers between 30 and 40.
Write your answers below.

Name _____

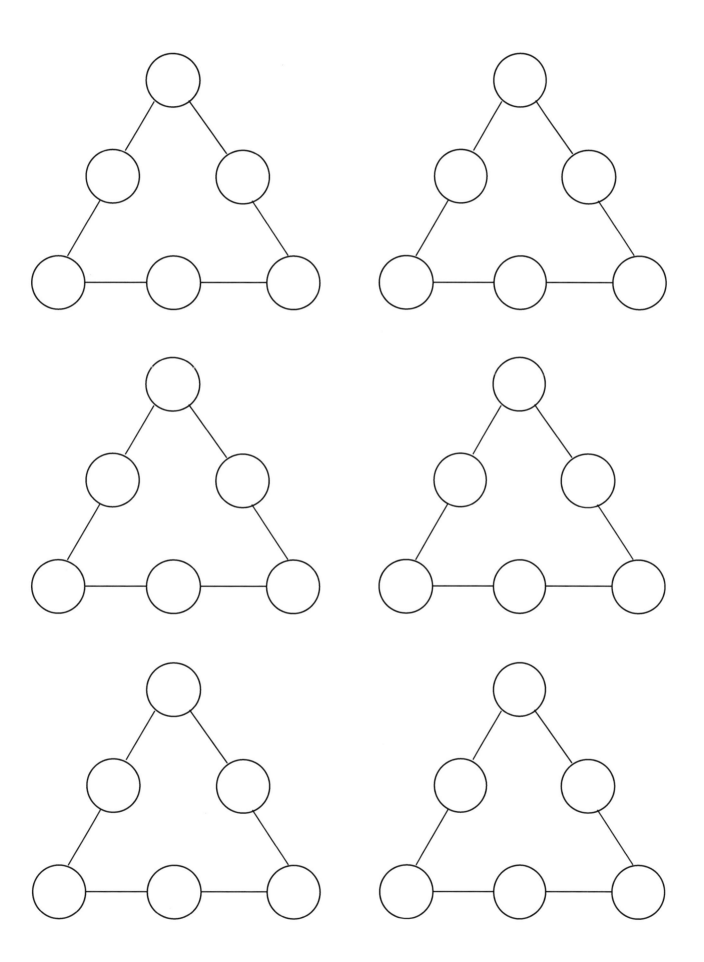

Name _____

Write some of your line totals in the left column and write the factors of each number in its row.

Name _____

1	2	3	4	5	6	7	8	9	10
11	12	13	14	15	16	17	18	19	20
21	22	23	24	25	26	27	28	29	30
31	32	33	34	35	36	37	38	39	40
41	42	43	44	45	46	47	48	49	50
51	52	53	54	55	56	57	58	59	60
61	62	63	64	65	66	67	68	69	70
71	72	73	74	75	76	77	78	79	80
81	82	83	84	85	86	87	88	89	90
91	92	93	94	95	96	97	98	99	100

Name _____

Find two answers for each of the following.

1. ☐ X ☐ X ☐ = 147 = ☐ X ☐ X ☐

2. ☐ X ☐ X ☐ = 144 = ☐ X ☐ X ☐

3. ☐ X ☐ X ☐ = 168 = ☐ X ☐ X ☐

4. ☐ X ☐ X ☐ = 126 = ☐ X ☐ X ☐

5. ☐ X ☐ X ☐ = 162 = ☐ X ☐ X ☐

6. ☐ X ☐ X ☐ = 125 = ☐ X ☐ X ☐

7. ☐ X ☐ X ☐ = 180 = ☐ X ☐ X ☐

8. ☐ X ☐ X ☐ = 128 = ☐ X ☐ X ☐

9. ☐ X ☐ X ☐ = 150 = ☐ X ☐ X ☐

10. ☐ X ☐ X ☐ = 108 = ☐ X ☐ X ☐

Name _____

Find two answers for each of the following.

1. $\boxed{7}$ X $\square$ X $\square$ = 147 = $\square$ X $\square$ X $\square$

2. $\square$ X $\square$ X $\square$ = 144 = $\square$ X $\boxed{12}$ X $\square$

3. $\square$ X $\square$ X $\boxed{4}$ = 168 = $\square$ X $\square$ X $\square$

4. $\square$ X $\square$ X $\square$ = 126 = $\square$ X $\boxed{9}$ X $\square$

5. $\square$ X $\boxed{6}$ X $\square$ = 162 = $\square$ X $\square$ X $\square$

6. $\square$ X $\boxed{5}$ X $\square$ = 125 = $\square$ X $\square$ X $\square$

7. $\square$ X $\square$ X $\square$ = 180 = $\square$ X $\square$ X $\boxed{4}$

8. $\square$ X $\square$ X $\square$ = 128 = $\boxed{8}$ X $\square$ X $\square$

9. $\boxed{3}$ X $\square$ X $\square$ = 150 = $\square$ X $\square$ X $\square$

10. $\square$ X $\square$ X $\boxed{9}$ = 108 = $\square$ X $\square$ X $\square$

Name _____

1. 3.8 =

2. 8.5 =

3. 6.5 =

4. 1.5714285 =

5. 4.3333333 =

6. 6.3333333 =

7. 1.4 =

8. 0.4117647 =

9. 0.1052631 =

10. 0.2941176 =

Name _____

1. $3.8 = 19 \div$

2. $8.5 = 17 \div$

3. $6.5 = 13 \div$

4. $1.5714285 = 11 \div$

5. $4.3333333 = 13 \div$

6. $6.3333333 = 19 \div$

7. $1.4 = 7 \div$

8. $0.4117647 = 7 \div$

9. $0.1052631 = 2 \div$

10. $0.2941176 = 5 \div$

Name _____

Tests of divisibility

A number can be divided exactly by 10, if the last digit is 0.

A number can be divided exactly by 2, if the last digit is 0, 2, 4, 6 or 8.

A number can be divided exactly by 3, if the sum of the digits is divisible by 3.

A number can be divided exactly by 4, if the last two digits are divisible by 4.

A number can be divided exactly by 5, if the last digit is 5 or 0.

A number can be divided exactly by 6, if the number is even and divisible by 3.

A number can be divided exactly by 8, if the last three digits can be divided by 8.

A number can be divided by 9, if the sum of the digits is divisible by 9.

A number can be divided exactly by 3, if the sum of the digits is divisible by 3.

A number can be divided exactly by 4, if the last two digits are divisible by 4.

A number can be divided exactly by 6, if the number is even and divisible by 3.

A number can be divided exactly by 8, if the last three digits can be divided by 8.

Name _____

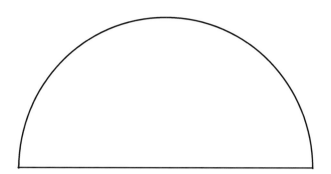
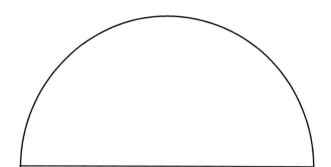
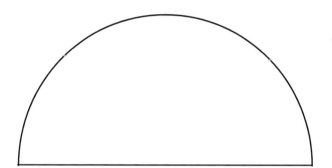
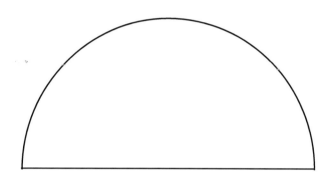
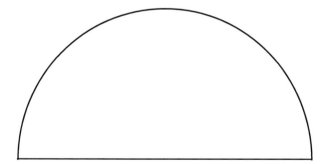
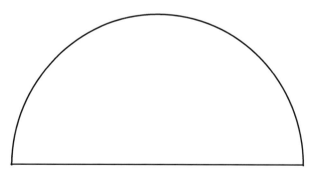

Name _____

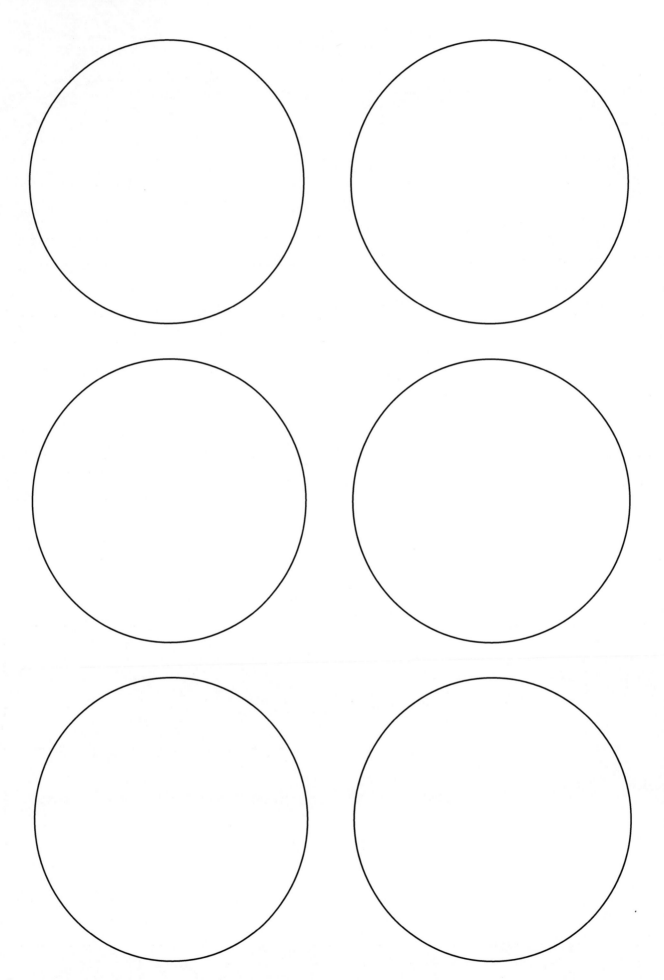

Name _____

If it is 9.17 am in London, it is the following times around the world.

Place	Time	Difference in hours and minutes
Los Angeles	01.17	
Chicago	03.17	
New York	04.17	
Buenos Aires	06.17	
Rome	10.17	
Istanbul	11.17	
Kuwait	12.17	
Kabul	13.17	
Delhi	14.47	
Rangoon	15.47	
Beijing	17.17	
Tokyo	18.17	
Canberra	19.17	
Wellington	21.17	
Hawaii	23.17	

Do any calculations here.

Name _____

Flight times from London to:
New York   2 hours 30 minutes
Rangoon   4 hours 10 minutes
Kuwait   2 hours
Wellington   8 hours 12 minutes
Delhi   6 hours 15 minutes

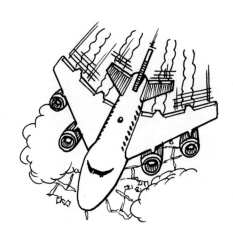

Answer the following questions.

What will local time be when the plane lands in New York if it takes off at:

1)   10.17?   _____

2)   13.17?   _____

3)   19.17?   _____

What will local time be when the plane lands in Rangoon if it takes off at:

4)   10.17?   _____

5)   11.17?   _____

6)   13.17?   _____

What will local time be when the plane lands in Kuwait if it takes off at:

7)   10.17?   _____

8)   11.59?   _____

9)   15.30?   _____

What will local time be when the plane lands in Wellington if it takes off at:

10)   10.17?   _____

11)   12.17?   _____

12)   15.30?   _____

What will local time be when the plane lands in Delhi if it takes off at:

13)   10.17?   _____

14)   14.17?   _____

15)   18.17?   _____

Name _____

For the international times activities, show your workings out in the boxes below.

1.

2.

3.

4.

5.

6.

Name _____

Flight times from London to:
New York   2 hours
Kabul   4 hours
Kuwait   3 hours
Wellington   8 hours

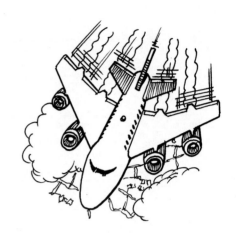

Answer the following questions.

What will local time be when the plane lands in New York if it takes off at:

1)   10.17?   _____

2)   13.17?   _____

3)   19.17?   _____

What will local time be when the plane lands in Kabul if it takes off at:

4)   10.17?   _____

5)   11.17?   _____

6)   13.17?   _____

What will local time be when the plane lands in Kuwait if it takes off at:

7)   10.17?   _____

8)   11.17?   _____

9)   15.17?   _____

What will local time be when the plane lands in Wellington if it takes off at:

10)   10.17?   _____

11)   12.17?   _____

12)   15.17?   _____

Name _____

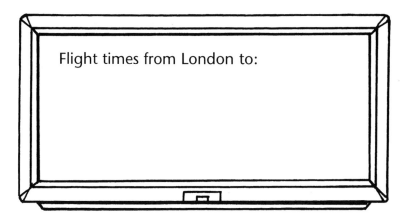

Flight times from London to:

Answer the following questions.

What will local time be when the plane lands in _____ if it takes off at:
1) _____
2) _____
3) _____

What will local time be when the plane lands in _____ if it takes off at:
4) _____
5) _____
6) _____

What will local time be when the plane lands in _____ if it takes off at:
7) _____
8) _____
9) _____

What will local time be when the plane lands in _____ if it takes off at:
10) _____
11) _____
12) _____

What will local time be when the plane lands in _____ if it takes off at:
13) _____
14) _____
15) _____

Name _____

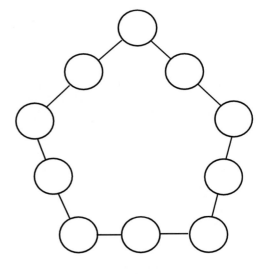

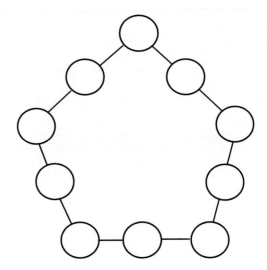

Name _____

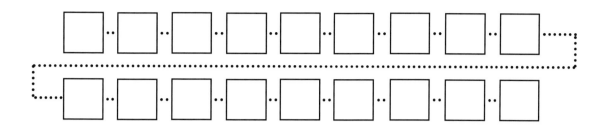

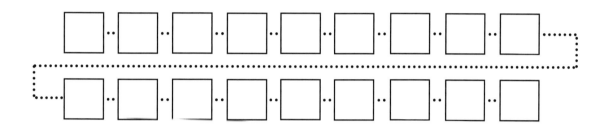

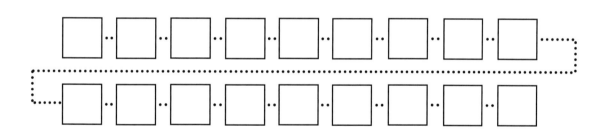

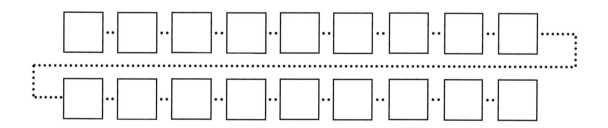

Name _____

Number	x10	x100	x1000
	÷10	÷100	÷1000

Name _____

Name _____

Name _____

Exit route	Distance and time taken

Notes